Machines As Big As Monsters

For Joanne Kellock

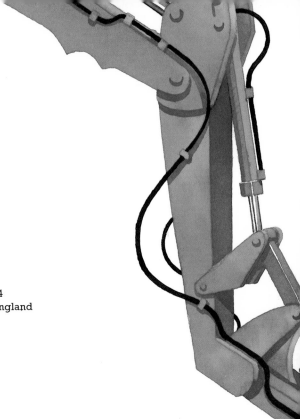

PUFFIN BOOKS
Published by the Penguin Group
Penguin Books USA Inc., 375 Hudson Street, New York, New York 10014
Penguin Books Ltd, Registered Offices: Harmondsworth, Middlesex, England
First published in the United Kingdom by Firefly Books Limited, 1989
Published by Puffin Books, a division of Penguin Books USA Inc., 1996
1   3   5   7   9   10   8   6   4   2
Copyright © Paul Stickland, 1989
Produced by Mathew Price Ltd.
The Old Glove Factory
Bristol Road
Sherborne
Dorset DT9 4HP
England
ISBN 0-14-055910-8
Printed in China

Machines As Big As Monsters

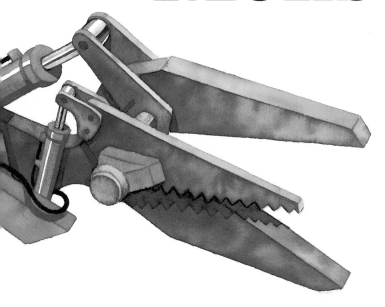

Paul Stickland

PUFFIN BOOKS

The Terex Titan is the largest dump truck in the world. It has ten wheels, each one as tall as three men. It has a huge diesel engine and can carry up to 350 tons. That's like carrying 175 elephants!

This giant floating crane is lowering the platform
of an oil rig into place. Tugboats help move
the floating crane from place to place.
Sometimes floating cranes are used
to rescue sunken ships.

This dragline excavator is digging a canal to bring
water through the desert. Each mouthful of sand
is at least as big as a car. Because the
excavator is so heavy, it moves on
caterpillar tracks instead of
wheels. The circular chain
treads keep the machine
from sinking into
the sand.

The gantry crane unloads heavy steel containers from ships. Sitting atop a rolling platform, the gantry crane moves from ship to ship along the edge of a harbor. Enormous cables wrap around pulleys to lift objects off the ground.

These excavators knock down old buildings to make room for new ones. First, the giant hydraulic shears of one excavator snap the concrete pillars like a nutcracker. Then, two other excavators smash the concrete into small pieces with their jackhammer heads.

This flying crane can carry a house up a mountain. After the house is built, the flying crane takes it up to the peak. Powered by a giant helicopter propeller, the flying crane can carry up to thirty tons.

The Galaxy C5 is the largest cargo aircraft in the world. When it is ready to be loaded, it sinks down on its twenty-eight wheels. Then, its nose is raised and its ramp is lowered. This plane is unloading sixteen giant trucks.

A space station is a place where astronauts can live in outer space. Inside the station, astronauts study the Earth from millions of miles away. Outside the station, the astronauts float around in zero gravity.

The bucket-wheel excavator is used for mining rocks. It scoops up rocks and dirt with revolving metal shovels and dumps them onto a conveyor belt. The belt carries the material to the opposite end of the machine, where a processor separates the rocks from the dirt and sorts the rocks by size for different purposes.

This strange-looking monster is a row of locks in a water barrier. The barrier controls the flow and level of water to protect cities from flooding, and the locks let ships pass through the barrier.

The chain-bucket dredger makes the water in a harbor deeper to allow ships to sail through. It scoops up soft sand from the harbor floor and pours it onto a barge. The barge then dumps the sand into the deep sea—or sometimes makes small islands.

The resurfacing machine repairs worn-out roads. First, a jackhammer breaks the surface of the road into small pieces. Next, the resurfacing machine picks the pieces up and grinds them into particles. Then, the new surface is spread out onto the road and rolled flat and smooth.

Glossary

astronauts people who travel in space

cable a strong rope usually made of metal wire

cargo the freight carried by a ship or plane

caterpillar tracks a pair of circular chain treads that helps heavy vehicles cross soft or very rough ground

conveyor belt a continuous moving belt driven by rollers that moves objects from one place to another

crane a machine for lifting and moving objects high off the ground

dredger a machine used to deepen harbors by scooping sand from the bottom

dump truck a heavy-duty truck that can tilt backward to dump loose material

harbor   a sheltered port for ships

jackhammer   a tool for breaking roads up into small pieces

lock   a gateway that lets ships pass through a barrier from one water level to another

pulley   a small wheel with a rope wrapped around its grooved rim, used to lift weights more easily

shears   a giant pair of scissors used for cutting heavy materials

space station   a large manned satellite designed for permanent orbit around Earth

tugboat   a small, powerful boat that helps to move large ships